At the wheel

Practicing the WH Sound

Timea Thompson

Rosen
PHONICS
READERS

Rosen
Classroom

My dad has a white truck.

There are four wheels.
Where are the wheels?

This is a wheel, too.
This wheel turns the car left
or right.

What other wheels can I find?
Where can I look?

This tractor has wheels.
What kind of wheels?

They are big wheels!

My sister shows me
three wheels.
Her wheels are different sizes.

8

Which wheel is the biggest?
Which wheels are the smallest?

My bike has wheels.
What color are the wheels?

The wheels are white!
I love my white wheels.

Which wheels do you like best?